LCR

To D

Here is

(it worked for Timbooktwo...)

In loving memory of our
own LCR -

Lydia Christina Rose

Tim
X

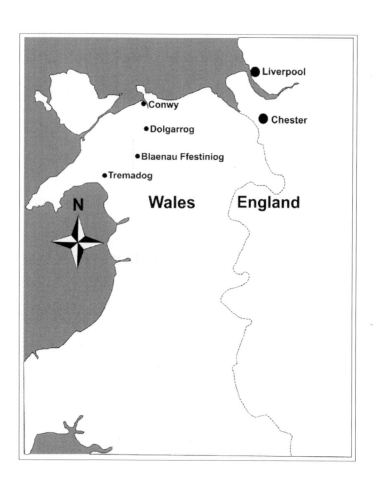

Introduction

'Lawrence of Arabia' is an Oscar-winning film which depicts T. E. Lawrence's heroic exploits in World War I, leading the Arab revolt, dressed in full Arabian costume and riding a camel bravely into battle.

Yet there is so much more to the man than this mere snapshot. Was his name Thomas Edward Lawrence or rather Thomas Edward Chapman or even John Hume Ross? L, C or R?

He famously wrote about the Seven Pillars of Wisdom and these form the structure of this tale.

Will Harry, Rob, Tom and Ted be able to unravel some of the mysteries where others have failed?

What was Lawrence really like? What were the secrets and inner thoughts of Lawrence of Tremadog, North Wales as he should have been called? How did his death save the lives of thousands and what was his true legacy? How did he really die? Read on with hope in your heart.

Proverbs Chapter 9 verse 1:

"Wisdom has built her home; she has set up its seven pillars."

Winston Churchill on Lawrence:

"He was clearly one of the greatest beings alive in this time."

Lawrence on dreams:

"All men dream, but not equally. Those who dream by night in the dusty recesses of their minds wake in the day to find that it was vanity; but the dreamers of the day are dangerous men, for they may act their dream with open eyes, to make it possible. This I did."

To my own LCR I dedicate Lawrence's poem:

'I loved you, so I drew these tides of men into my hands and wrote my will across the sky in stars.
To earn you freedom, the seven pillared worthy house, that your eyes might be shining for me
When we came.
Death seemed my servant on the road, till we were near and saw you waiting.
When you smiled, and in sorrowful entry he outran me and took you apart; into his quietness.'

How I miss you...

1

"Dad, do you know anything about the Seven Pillars of Wisdom?"

Ted, the long-suffering father, had grown accustomed to his son Tom's never-ending stream of questions, but they had certainly got trickier over the years and come a long way from, 'Are we there yet?' and 'Why do I always have to go to bed first?'

As a teacher of some thirty years, Ted had learnt how to bluff his way out of most situations, but since the advent of Google and the immediacy of iPhones he was more wary of being caught out, so he fended it off with a question of his own.

"Why do you ask? Surely you're not doing history coursework on holiday?"

He pinched himself hard.

"Wake up Ted! You must be dreaming!"

"Cut out the sarcasm. My English teacher Miss Wood told us it's supposed to be the lowest form of wit, though she also said on my report: 'Tom thinks he's a wit, but he's only half right.'"

Ted smiled at the memory. His own pièce de résistance in report writing had been:

"Michael reminds me of Van Gogh in the classroom. Whatever I say to him goes in one ear - and straight out of the same ear."

It had been deleted by his SLT line manager before the parents could start proceedings.

"There's a bench in the garden with seven pillars carved into it and a bible verse from Proverbs about building a house of seven pillars."

"Go and Google it. My genius levels are running rather low at the moment."

Tom wandered off into the front room and Ted watched him go. He had been unsure whether a summer holiday in North Wales, with all its fond but painful memories, was a good idea but the lads seemed to be coping.

Harry, the eldest, was forever organising and busying himself with projects - almost in denial, or more likely his own coping mechanism.

Rob had been the really angry one, but it only came in waves now, and he was as active as ever, going for runs and challenging the locals in the park in Porthmadog to a footy match.

Tom was full of questions as always. Questions he couldn't answer and ones which kept him awake at night - every night.

Tremadog was a lovely place to spend a week. There were lots to see and do on the Llyn Peninsula and he was so proud of his sons. If only Rosie were here it would be perfect...

Perhaps the Seven Pillars of Wisdom would hold the key and help him rebuild his own life.

2

Ted had chosen Snowdon Lodge partly because of its location, conveniently situated near to the mountains of Snowdonia and the coast of the Llyn Peninsula, but mainly because of its historical links as the birthplace of Lawrence of Arabia. The whole family were fascinated by history so it almost seemed too good to be true to sleep under the same roof as such an influential figure.

Tom had been as curious as ever. Why was he called Lawrence of Arabia if he was born in Tremadog? Why was he even called by the surname of Lawrence in the first place if his dad was Sir Thomas Chapman and they always took their father's name in those days? Shouldn't he be known as Chapman of Tremadog? Not quite as romantic sounding but more accurate surely?

They spent the evening sharing a Chinese take away from the Happy Chop Suey House in the High Street, arguing about the itinerary for the week ahead.

Seven days was clearly not going to be long enough to pack in all they wanted to do. Harry wanted to visit all the castles nearby, particularly Caernarfon and Criccieth and go on the steam railways.

Rob, the active one, wanted to experience Bounce Below, 'The World's First Subterranean playground', do the fastest zip line in the world and climb Snowdon by the six major routes all before breakfast on day one!

Tom wanted to go surfing at the new Surf Snowdonia attraction and find out as much as he possibly could about Lawrence of Arabia so that he could quiz Mr Roberts, his history teacher, when he got back to school.

Ted was forced to play mediator and introduce the scandalous concept of a budget. Walking up Snowdon was clearly the cheapest option, but zip wires, surfing and bouncing sounded fantastic - but expensive. They would have to plan carefully, weigh up the options and cost them properly if they weren't to run out of money by Tuesday. Prudence was needed - wise decisions tempered with self-restraint and an element of caution.

The first pillar of their seven day adventure was in place and after more discussions and highly competitive games of Taboo and Cranium the lads finally agreed to go to bed.

Ted decided to google "prudence" before he retired. It was a word he had heard used only occasionally; in fact it always reminded him of playing his Alvarez guitar strumming 'Dear Prudence' and singing the chorus "Round, round, round, round, round. Round, round, round, round, round. Look around." Lennon and McCartney had such a way with words!

Dictionary.com defined prudence as "care, caution and self-restraint and wisdom in looking ahead."

He headed for bed, praying that he would be spared the horrible flashbacks and horrific nightmares he had been plagued by since he lost Rosie in April.

His mind drifted between thoughts of the holiday ahead; reminiscences of happy times and images of Peter O'Toole as Lawrence of Arabia muttering "prudence, prudence" at war counsels with Arab chiefs and British army officers.

3

Ted had researched dreams in great depth and detail since April and discovered that everybody dreams on average four to six times a night, though not many people remember them.

Dreams of falling, or sinking, or being chased were the most common and psychoanalysts interpreted these fears in many and varied ways.

Ted had vivid memories of two separate dreams that first night in Tremadog. In the first he was a greylag goose flying at the front of a gaggle of geese which consisted of his family. He was leading the way and they were obviously migrating and heading for sunnier climes. He was struggling against the strong headwinds and stormy weather and was tempted to land and shelter, but he knew that the short-term pain was for long-term gain and he had to soldier on for the sake of his family and friends who were willing him on, though they realised how hard it was for him.

He glanced back and saw his three lads and a whole group of family and friends flying behind him, almost pushing him forward, but as he looked for Rosie, his wife, he realised she was not there. He awoke with a shiver.

When he finally got off to sleep again he had an even more vivid dream. He was at the funeral of Lawrence of Arabia, just like at the start of the film. A journalist was stopping mourners as they came out of the service and asking them what they knew about Lawrence.

Suddenly he felt a tug on his arm and a mysterious-looking stranger took him to one side. He was small in stature - about five feet five inches tall and had a haunted look with sunken eyes which were constantly darting to and fro, as if searching for an unseen enemy.

"All this fuss - I told them I wanted a quiet burial in Dorset, not the world and his wife paying tribute. I told the king the same in October 1918 when they offered me a knighthood. Sir Thomas Edward

Lawrence they wanted to call me and that's not even my real name.

My father was Sir Thomas Chapman so I should have taken his name if it hadn't been for all the scandal of being born out of wedlock to an aristocrat and his 18 year old governess.

I didn't choose my parents, but what a start to life that was! I was always on the move - from Tremadog where I was born, to Cornwall, Scotland, The Channel Islands and then finally Oxford.

No wonder I enjoyed travelling and never really settled anywhere. I hated school and being told what to do and what to study. It was irrelevant, time-wasting and a nuisance and I filled my time reading about crusading knights and visiting museums and churches in Oxford with my best friend Cyril. We particularly enjoyed making brass rubbings and collecting pottery, coins and anything of historical significance.

Sometimes we paid and bartered for them - sometimes we helped ourselves. They were happy days; mainly because we had plenty of freedom.

It was the same at University. I went to Jesus College and managed to fluke a first class honours degree by making up my own syllabus and producing a thesis on medieval military history. I had countless arguments with my private tutor, L. C. Jane and had to learn to be more diplomatic, more cautious, wiser and more prudent.

Money was never a problem during my days in Oxford, but I could easily have gone wild and abused my position of privilege.

I had to learn self-restraint and to consider the consequences of my actions. Stealing from churches and museums was wrong, I knew that, but I got away with it. But what if I got caught?

Arguing with teachers and academics at school and university was good fun - but where would it get me if I was expelled or sent down from Jesus College? I needed the qualifications to open up more opportunities so self-restraint, common sense and prudence became the first pillar to build my future on."

4

Ted had woken up with a jolt, muttering the word "prudence" over and over.

At breakfast he wondered whether he should share his dreams with Harry, Rob and Tom, but decided that he would keep them to himself so as not to spoil the day and maybe bring them into conversation that evening.

He did share with Tom his research into the meaning of prudence, not daring to mention the insight given to him personally by Lawrence of Arabia himself! They would have thought he had been on the whisky again…

Day One he decided was to be Prudence Monday; an interesting concept as the boys had chosen Blaenau Ffestiniog as their first destination with an educational tour of the Llechwedd Slate Caverns to keep their teacher/dad happy and Bounce Below and Zip World to satisfy the adrenaline junkies.

Ted insisted wisely that they took the tour first, so the brothers had to learn self-restraint as they travelled along the Miners' Tramway 800 metres underground and learnt all about the history of slate quarrying in the area.

It was genuinely very interesting, but they couldn't wait for it to finish so they could get to the more exciting part of the day.

Ted retired to the cafe to "look after the bags" and watched in fascination as Harry, Rob and Tom took to the "subterranean playground."

They were so different in character and yet all from the same genes and upbringing. Harry carefully checked his safety equipment, tightening his hard hat and tucking his jeans into his trainers and making sure all his body was covered. He watched for a while as other youngsters plunged down the slides, tunnels and nets.

Rob looked for somebody of similar ability to race against. He challenged an older teenager to see who could get fastest around the course and was a blur as he jumped, climbed and slid his way around.

Tom wanted to try everything immediately. His hat wasn't properly fastened so it came off as he landed. As he negotiated one of the faster slides his trousers rode up and he ended up with scratches down the sides of his legs. He had a whale of a time but wished he had been more cautious and he wouldn't have got so many cuts and bruises.

They all agreed it was awesome, but wished they had listened more intently to the safety lecture and promotional video before they had learnt the hard way.

As they hobbled and limped their way to the cafe to meet up with dad they voted on "Wipeout of the Day" and Tom was the unanimous winner, falling off the balance beam and landing heavily with one leg either side.

"We need more sopranos on the Kop," joked Tom, "to sing 'You'll never walk again.'"

Ted was glad they'd had such a great time and that a trip to A&E had been avoided this time, but he couldn't help commenting:

"Prudence Monday. If only you'd all followed the example of your big brother and been more cautious and self-restrained you wouldn't be last in the race for the car…"

His words trailed off as he shot out of the door and was indeed first to touch the car; followed by Harry, a hobbling Rob and a tenderly tip-toeing Tom

5

"Tonight's à la carte Michelin-starred dish of the day is poisson frit accompanied by sglodion and erbsen püree," Ted announced.

"Great…fish, chips and mushy peas are my favourite!"

Ted's attempts to hide the gastronomic delights of the evening by combining French, Welsh and German fell on deaf ears as usual.

They were used to their dad's "jokes" and the takeaway bag labelled 'Chippy Dre, Tremadog' was also a clue that even Inspector Clouseau would have worked out.

"Great day dad, thanks. Bounce Below and Zip World were awesome… and the Slate Caverns too of course." Rob was first to speak as usual.

"Even better if mum had been there to share it with us…" Tom's words were followed by a void of silence with Harry looking away angrily, Rob staring into space and Ted wiping away a tear.

It seemed the perfect moment to share his dreams. He described in detail the geese migration story, interrupted only by Tom's murmurings of "It would be cool to fly" and "How do birds know which way to go?"

Rob couldn't resist the retort of, "they go on twitter and another bird tweets the answer."

Harry silenced them both with his withering teacher's stare.

At the end of the story Harry, who had reacted with anger and bitterness to his mum's illness and sudden death, couldn't help commenting,

"But will it ever be really sunny again? What's the point anyway? We may as well land and stop pretending."

Ted had gone through the same emotions himself and empathised, but knew he had to respond.

"But that's not what she would have wanted. Remember the poem at the funeral - you can cry and close your mind, be empty and turn your back or you can do what she'd want; smile, open your eyes, love and go on."

"But it's too hard…" Harry's voice quivered.

After an agonisingly long silence Tom asked:

"Where do you think mum was in your dream? It would be so much easier if we knew where she was now."

Ted put his arm around Tom's shoulders.

"We've got to believe that she's gone to a better place. There must be a reason why she was taken. I did sense her flying with us, though we couldn't see her, just as we all feel her presence every day. It reminded me of that song 'Wind beneath my wings.' Mum was always happy to let us have the glory while she walked behind; picking up the washing, tidying up and providing strength for all of us."

Time to change the subject, Ted thought.

"I had another dream too - about Lawrence of Arabia and Prudence."

The boys were silent as he recounted his second dream, but full of questions when he had finished.

"How can anyone turn down a knighthood? I hope I get one for footy, like Sir Stanley Matthews and Sir Bobby Moore and Sir Jordan Henderson, when he captains us to the League title ten years in a row." Rob's optimism had returned with a bang.

"All anyone knows about Lawrence comes from that Peter O'Toole film and that's even more ridiculous when you think O'Toole was well over six feet and Lawrence was only 5'5."

"I agree with him about school though. If it wasn't for break and lunch time footy it would be a total waste of time."

Rob's one track mind was off again.

"What about Prudence?" Tom asked. "Today was supposed to be Prudence Monday, so what have we learned?"

"I've learnt to be cautious and not take stupid risks," Harry interjected.

"and I've learnt that you can actually cry with laughter when your baby bro' does the splits over the balance beam."

He broke into a soprano version of Aled Jones' 'Walking in the Air'.

"And I've learnt to look before you leap and many hands make light work but too many cooks can spoil the broth."

Ted smiled. He too had learnt a lot about Lawrence of Arabia, Prudence, his family and himself. What would Tuesday hold - or more importantly what would Monday night's dreams hold?

He packed the boys off to bed and raided the kitchen for as much cheddar cheese washed down with milk and whisky as he could find, to ensure his serotonin and tryptophan levels were at maximum overload level. Dream on!

6

Sure enough, the cocktail of cheese, milk and whisky did the trick and Ted slept soundly and dreamed vividly, though he did wake up with a banging headache.

In his first dream he was a butterfly trapped in a cocoon and fighting desperately to get out. Day after day he fought long and hard but was seemingly getting nowhere and at the end of each day he collapsed with exhaustion and depression.

Outside the cocoon he could see all his friends and family urging him on, but it frustrated him and saddened him that none of them actually, physically helped by pulling the cocoon apart and setting him free to fly.

He was close to giving up so many times, but finally on a bright summer's day he emerged, flexed and stretched his wings and was ready to fly.

One burning question had to be answered before he did. "Why didn't you help me earlier? Why did you just stand by and watch?"

It was only then that his friends and family explained that it was God's plan as it was only by building up his strength in the cocoon by fighting to escape that the wings fully developed. If they had stepped in earlier, the results could have been catastrophic.

In his second dream, Lawrence appeared again and continued his autobiographical account.

"The second pillar of wisdom that I had to learn," he said "was knowledge and discretion. I had to learn the importance of planning and using knowledge gained to look ahead.

This was brought home to me most dramatically during my first real adventure which was during the summer holiday at the end of my first year at Oxford University.

I had never really felt settled anywhere after all the moves as a child so I suppose I developed a real wanderlust which was to haunt me all of my life.

The summer was long. I had no ties and a bicycle, so I set off for France. I didn't know where I was going to go, what I was going to see and where I was going to sleep, but determination drove me forward and off I went.

Between the middle of July and early September I rode over 2,400 miles from Calais in the north, through Vézélay with its Norman basilica, Arles with its twelfth century monastery, Agde with its stunning black basalt cathedral, through beautiful and unforgettable Carcassonne, ever southward.

I saw some amazing sights; the highlight being the Gothic cathedral of Notre-Dame at Chartres but wasted so much time zigzagging across country because I hadn't planned my route and just went where the whim took me.

Chartres Cathedral was my first truly religious experience as I felt that I had glimpsed heaven and the glory of God and it was really exciting and inspirational.

I was so glad to be alive, riding fifty to sixty miles every day on a diet of bread, milk and fruit and sleeping under the stars, free and fulfilled.

Finally, after the wonders of the Crusader castle at Aigues-Mortes, I saw the Mediterranean and ran to bathe in its dancing ripples.

This was the end of this journey, but I knew it was only the start of my life's journey and as I gazed out to sea I knew ahead lay Greece, Carthage, Tyre, Syria, Italy, Spain, Sicily, Crete…the list was endless and I was determined to see them, but plan properly next time.

I would gather knowledge, discern the way forward and plan accordingly. The second pillar of wisdom was firmly entrenched in my life."

7

"To fail to plan, is to plan to fail." Ted was using his best teacher's voice to get the attention of his sons during breakfast the following morning. "Give it a rest dad. We're on holiday. You'll be drawing up a mind map next and telling us what our WALTs and WILFs are."

"Funnily enough, you're spot on Rob. Our WALT - what we are learning today -is the importance of prior knowledge and planning. Our WILF - what I am looking for - is the top of the highest mountain in Wales. Yr Wyddfa the Welsh call it, but Snowdon to you and me. 3560 feet above sea level and today's supposed to be the clearest day weather-wise, so onwards and upwards."

"But I thought we were meant to plan before we set off," Harry reasoned.

"Quite right. You're all old enough to cope on your own now - even you Tom, so we are going to take four different paths up and see who gets there first. Oh, by the way - the train is banned!"

Harry, Rob and Tom - as competitive as ever - were excited at the prospect.

"There are four route maps here, face down. They are for the Llanberis, Snowdon Ranger, Miners' and Pyg Tracks. You will each pick one and I'll have the last one. There is also a bus timetable and £10 spending money. We will meet in the cafe at the top. Spend as long as you want preparing and planning, but remember it's a race. Don't take any stupid risks and all four of these paths are perfectly safe. I deliberately haven't included the Watkin Path or Rhyd Ddu because those are dodgy in places. Any questions anyone?"

Tom had hundreds but now wasn't the time. The lads scurried off to their bedrooms to plan and pack after grabbing one of the route maps from the pile.

. . .

Four hours later Ted pushed open the heavy wooden doors of Hafod Eryri, the summit cafe, to be greeted by two grinning sons.

"Bronze - not bad for an old timer," commented Harry.

"Who was here first?"

"Me, of course, brains always did defeat brawn. Wonder where Rob is? You did tell him Snowdon and not Ben Nevis?"

"He sent me a text about ten minutes ago to say he was running up the Miners' Track and wouldn't be too long. He said he'd had some difficulties en route. I can't wait to hear his excuses."

"O.K. Gold Medal winner – first - Harry tell us your version."

"Well I picked the Llanberis Path so I googled it and found out it was the longest, but less steep of all the paths. I checked the bus timetable but there wasn't one to Llanberis for a couple of hours, so I phoned for a taxi - £9, so within budget - and spent the fifteen minute wait researching my route and packing my backpack. Apparently the annual Snowdon Race follows that route and the record is 39 minutes so as long as I kept up a steady pace I knew I was in with a chance. It wasn't a particularly interesting climb, but it was easy and I beat Tom by about twenty minutes and you by forty."

"Silver goes to Tom, what about you? I got Snowdon Ranger, Rob's on the Miners' Track so you must have drawn the Pyg Track."

"Yep, that's right. Unlike Harry my bus was to Pen-y-Pass and it was the second one due, so only twenty minutes to wait. I had a quick look at the map then headed down to the shops for provisions - Red Bull and Kendal Mint Cake they recommended. The path was steep in places but I avoided Crib Goch which looked decidedly dodgy and got here second. I took some ace pictures of standing stones and views over the lake."

Next Ted told his account.

"I slipped out the back to where I'd hidden the car last night, checked the map and headed for the youth hostel near Llyn Cwellyn where the path starts. I must have been way ahead of you at that stage, but all the zigzags and ridge walking took it out of me and I had to rest a few times. The views were amazing and third's not bad…for an old timer!"

"Loser! Loser!" even Ted couldn't help joining in.

"We thought you were the favourite Rob, county athlete, super-fit, six-packed soccer star. What happened?"

"My plan was to prove you didn't need a plan. I grabbed the Miners' Track guide and ran straight out of the door to the bus stop. A bus was just coming round the corner so I jumped on, hardly believing my luck. I wasn't sure where I was headed so I asked the driver if he was going to Miners and he looked confused, but said yes.

It was a longer journey than I thought but he finally pointed to a sign and said. 'Here you go son - Menai.' It was some place called Menai Bridge.

I had no idea where I was so I tried to hitch a lift back, but everybody just laughed when they saw the sign I had made saying 'Summit of Snowdon'.

Eventually a farmer picked me up and I sat in the back of his tractor for what seemed like hours. He told me I had about an hour's walk from there to the car park at Pen-y-Pass and from there I ran all the way up.

Unlucky wasn't I?"

He glanced round at his brothers and dad who were open-mouthed with astonishment.

"After three lads," said Ted. "1, 2, 3 - to fail to plan is to plan to fail!" they chorused.

"Rob - the ice-creams are on you."

8

Evening meal was quieter than usual. A combination of the fresh air and brisk exercise had taken its toll on all four of them.

Ted had been forced to have a nap when they got back to the Lodge while Harry had been left in charge of ordering the takeaway.

His favourite was Indian so Sima Tandoori was chosen and Ted woke up to the aromas of Chicken Madras and Beef Madras, Lamb Rogan Josh, Prawn Vindaloo and Beef Masala. As he walked into the dining room, Rob did his best Susan Boyle impression singing:

"I dreamed a dream in time gone by

I was a goose and I was flying…"

"Come on dad. In all the excitement of today you've not told us the latest instalment."

"Funnily enough, there were two again I can remember."

He recounted first the butterfly story and the three lads sat attentively listening.

"We did that in Science at school," Harry commented. "It is true. There's even a speeded up version of it on YouTube you can watch. But what does it mean?"

"Well I think we're all stuck in a cocoon at the moment and trying desperately to break out. The thing is we've all got to give it time and let our wings develop. Mum only died four months ago and things will never be the same - but they can be, and must be good."

The three lads stared into space. They knew what their dad was saying was common sense, but shock, grief and anger were an explosive mixture and there was clearly no easy answer.

Harry had tried alcohol to drown his sorrows - that only made it worse. Ted had been recommended heavy-duty tranquilizers to help him sleep, hypnosis to help him cope and every therapy known to man, but they had all proved useless. The fact was that

Rosie was gone - wife, mum, sister, friend, teacher to so many and somehow they had to move forward without her.

Tom was the first to break the silence:

"What about your second dream? Was it about Lawrence of Arabia again?"

"Yes and the second pillar of wisdom."

He told them Lawrence's version of his cycling trip to France and again they listened spellbound.

"Thought he was an intelligent bloke - fancy setting off like that with no real plan. Asking for trouble…"

His two brothers and dad were struck by the sheer irony of his comments considering Rob's performance in the Snowdon Challenge.

"The most important thing is, that he learned a lesson and vowed never to make the same mistake again. So next time Rob…"

"But what if we can't plan? Nobody expected the world to plunge into war in 1914 and that must have scuppered any plans Lawrence had after he left university." Harry always asked the telling, most challenging questions.

"Then we have to deal with it. Nobody could foresee or plan for what has happened in our family since last year's holiday in Denbigh. Nobody knew your mum was ill then. Nobody spotted the vasculitis until it was too late. Nobody could possibly predict the brain haemorrhage…"

Each forbidden word - vasculitis - haemorrhage - was like a hammer blow to each one of them. They had agreed as a family to talk things through rather than bottle them up like a volcano waiting to erupt, but this was tough. They had decided together to fund-raise for Vasculitis UK so an early intervention; a cure could be found - but what about now?

"The second pillar of wisdom is knowledge and direction; the importance of planning. All our previous plans are in ruins, but we've somehow got to 'go again'. We all feel like giving up and bemoaning our lot but we simply can't. There are going to be plenty of horrendous days, but lots of good ones too. Like today."

All three of the boys nodded and opted for a change of subject.

"Wednesday tomorrow, Hump Day, Miss Powell calls it. I wonder what it has in store?"

9

'The third pillar of wisdom', he had read just before going to bed, 'is fear of God and hating evil'.

Not exactly a recipe for sweet slumbers, Ted thought, but certainly thought-provoking.

He had believed in God all his life, but this had been really shaken in the last six months. He had heard all the challenging questions that atheists and agnostics had posed.

'If there is a God - why does He allow suffering? Why does He allow wars to happen? Why didn't He stop the tsunami? Why doesn't He step in to stop evil-doers and paedophiles and murderers?"

To those he now had to add; 'Why my family? Why isn't there a cure for vasculitis? Why do some less worthy people live longer than those who have so much to give?'

As he drifted off to sleep he was reminded of his dear friends Mavis and Denis who had prayed long and hard for healing, but unsuccessfully seemingly. Reverend Pam's explanation that their prayers had been answered, and Rosie's suffering had ended and she had been healed forever, had blown his mind. He could see the logic in it, but now hundreds of others were suffering too…

In his dream he saw some ducklings on a pond learning to swim. They were splashing around having fun and enjoying their new-found freedom.

Suddenly one of them got trapped in the reeds and started flapping its wings and quacking frantically. The mother duck saw the problem and swam quickly over to rescue its offspring.

After that, the duckling was too frightened of the water and its dangers to swim. The rest of the ducklings swam off early every day and came back with stories of their adventures and escapades, but to no avail. Their brother was too scared.

A few weeks later the duckling had grown bigger and stronger but was still sitting on the bank refusing to swim.

Another group of ducklings passed and exactly the same thing happened, but this time the mother duck was too far away and didn't hear the squawks for help.

A buzzard began circling overhead and the duck knew he had a choice. If he did nothing, the buzzard would pounce and the duckling would be on the menu, but if he overcame his fear he could rescue him and all would be well.

Instinctively he made the decision and plunged into the water and it only took seconds to release the duckling.

Suddenly he realised he was in the water and swimming again - it felt good! He had conquered his fear and now could live life to the full.

The second dream was about Lawrence again and equally dramatic.

10

Lawrence told him about his second summer adventure:

"After my taster in France I was determined to learn from my mistakes and plan the following year's adventure more thoroughly.

I had struck up an acquaintance with Charles Bell the Assistant Director of the Ashmolean Museum in Oxford and he suggested I combined my degree study with my travels to research the Holy Land's churches and castles, to settle the argument of whether the East influenced the West, or the West led the East.

This sparked my imagination and I spent months writing to travellers and historians like Charles Doughty and David Hogarth.

They gave me sound advice, though both thought that travelling in the heat of summer and on my own were too dangerous.

This I chose to ignore, so on July 5th 1909, wearing a lightweight suit, into which I had sewn extra pockets to carry my papers, and a fine woollen shirt, I walked out of Beirut towards Sidon.

There was money in my pocket and a Mauser pistol in my bag. I didn't have a care in the world and was really excited about the prospects. What could possibly go wrong? I had no worries, no fears.

Sidon was beautiful. It had a natural harbour with streets so narrow that two people could hardly pass. There was an incredibly impressive castle built on a mound of purple shells and endless treasures to discover and examine.

From Sidon I headed ever south, a week's long trek into Galilee and a town called Nabatieh. I had hired a guide and interpreter and found the locals extremely friendly and hospitable.

From there I walked south from Damascus to Palestine lined with brooding medieval castle towers. This was the place of my childhood dreams; of courtly knights, chainmail and armour.

The road, or more correctly track, wound its way through a series of valleys through surprisingly fertile hills and, though the heat was intense, the views of snow-capped Mount Hermon and the mountains of Bashan were a sight to behold.

My next stop was Banais, a heavily fortified town at the source of the Jordan River, a Crusader stronghold and fascinating place. Here I was happy to stay for a few days to rest and recuperate, then onwards to Safed, high in the lush Galilee hills.

There I was greeted by Doctor Anderson and his English wife and four children who looked after me so well that I was tempted to stay and holiday, rather than continue my journey.

From Safed I walked south through real Bible territory - Capernaum, Lake Tiberias, Galilee and Tyre. I really felt that I was following the footsteps of Jesus.

Tiberias was the furthest south I intended to go and from there I walked across Galilee to the Mediterranean Coast and on to Acre, then completed my circuit and after six long weeks I was back in Beirut. I had averaged twenty two miles a day - thirty six on one challenging day - and was exhausted, but exhilarated.

It was time to rest and recharge the batteries before the northern assault.

11

"On 6th August 1909 I headed out of Beirut, crossing the Dog River and reaching Jebail, with its two castles and impressive churches.

I met an American missionary called Miss Holmes who begged me to stay and help, warning me of the dangers of travelling on foot, on my own, to the north.

I enjoyed her company but had no fear of what lay ahead so travelled on. My movement was slower, partly because of contracting malaria and partly the state of the roads.

Tripoli was an interesting stop, but if I was to complete my route by the end of September to be back for the start of term, I had to keep moving. It was approximately three weeks to Aleppi, another week to Edessa and about ten days to return to Damascus.

I celebrated my 21st birthday in the perfect way - alone, my bag on my back, above Tripoli with superb views in every direction.

Crac des Chevaliers Castle was my favourite. It had a splendid Arab gateway leading into an impressive courtyard and keep. I truly felt like a Crusader King.

There were so many unforgettable sights on that journey - Safita, Latakia and Qadmas to name but three.

I was also attacked for the first time by an Arab with an old gun who threatened me and shot at me, though he soon thought better of it when I fired my Mauser over his head as a warning shot.

This was my first real alarm, but it did not deter me, as fear was not part of my nature, so I journeyed on, via Sahyun and on to Aleppo.

Aleppo was home to more than 200,000 people with a real mix of Muslims, Christians, Syrians, Kurds, Greeks and Armenians - a hotbed of violence; so my stay was brief.

I wanted to explore the antiquities and treasures of Bashar and was not to be deterred.

At Seruj my adventure ended. I was attacked and robbed in the middle of the night and rushed to hospital with such horrific injuries that an Aleppo newspaper were so convinced that they were fatal, that they reported my "murder" in the following day's edition.

I was terrified. A group of Kurds had heard of my arrival "carrying many treasures" and were so enraged by their pathetic haul of coins, pottery and trinkets that they beat me up and left me for dead.

I had been warned by so many people before and after my journey about the dangers, but had no fear - an almost fatal mistake.

At any rate my adventure was over I lied to my parents that I was coming home early "for lack of money" and returned to Damascus by train when I was fit enough to travel, then on to Beirut and home to England by boat.

It would take time for my physical wounds to heal, but the scars would go deeper.

A healthy fear and respect for my surroundings and culture would be ingrained in me forever."

12

Breakfast was cereal, sausage baps and bacon butties, washed down with tea, coffee and orange juice.

"The third pillar of wisdom and Wednesday's focus is fear of God, having reverence and hating evil."

The three lads were perplexed as to how this could possibly be built into Day 3 of their North Wales holiday.

"So - you survived Bounce Below and the zip wires in the caverns; you all made it to the top of Snowdon - eventually; but today is the ultimate challenge and test of nerve. I'll be doing the really dangerous bit; looking after the bags in the coffee shop, while you three experience the nearest thing to flying - Zip World in Bethesda."

"Wow, thanks dad! Friends from school went over Easter and they said

it was awesome."

Rob was back in Statto mode.

"The longest zip line in Europe, the fastest in the world. Descent from 1500 feet, riders can exceed 100 miles per hour."

Ted was fascinated by his sons' reactions in the car as they drove to Bethesda. Harry was quiet and thoughtful, Tom was full of questions and wanted more detail, whereas Rob was buzzing with excitement and couldn't wait to get started.

He thought about Lawrence's adventures he had dreamed about and wondered which of his offspring was most like him.

Maybe if you took the studious, intellectual attitude of Harry, added the questioning, explorative nature of Tom and then threw in the sheer energy and enthusiasm of Rob you would be close.

He wasn't sure how they would react when they actually saw the scariness of the ride and made a mental note to check on all three before they hurtled into the distance.

As it was, he had nothing to worry about with Harry. He checked, double-checked and in fact quintuple-checked every knot and piece of safety equipment.

It was the same with Tom. He asked so many questions that he was assigned his very own instructor who went through everything step by step.

Rob was different. He was in such a rush to get going that he had left before Ted got there and had joined up with another group as you had to be in a group of four.

Ted left his mobile number at the desk, signed the consent form and headed for the cafe, fingers crossed.

He was halfway through his cappuccino when his mobile rang. At first he thought it was one of the lads prank-calling him, but no, it was one of the centre leaders asking him to go to the main desk at once.

Ted felt sick as he ran to the office. Flashbacks of his dream kept replaying in his mind and his new-found pessimism returned with a vengeance.

He was led silently to the rear office and there was Rob - no cuts, no bruises, no life-threatening injuries, just sitting in the corner quivering with fear.

"Dad! Dad! Thank God! Don't let them force me to do it. It's bonkers! My boxers were white this morning, but I think they're a dark shade of brown now."

Ted smiled - more in relief than anything and hugged Rob.

"Thank goodness you're safe. I thought…" His voice trailed away.

"I'm fine now - but can we go please? Please!"

As they filed away Rob shuddered as he looked at all the pictures of the daredevil riders descending the wire.

They went to the cafe to wait for the others and Ted was surprised, and delighted, when the usually undemonstrative Rob snuggled into him and motioned that he wanted to whisper something in his dad's ear.

Would it be a mumbled "Thanks" or "Love you", but no - "promise you won't tell the others. They'll take the mick for ages."

13

Wednesday's evening meal was a lively and raucous affair. Pizzas had been ordered in and delivered from Porthmadog and the lads were in a boisterous mood. Harry and Tom were full of enthusiasm about their adventurous trip to Bethesda - and Rob was doing a good job of pretending to be.

Fortunately he had last been seen by the other two dashing off with a prior group, so the fact that he was waiting for them in the cafe with dad when they finished, made perfect sense.

Ted had decided to honour his promise and keep it as an ace up his sleeve for a future occasion.

"Right, dad, we'll close our eyes and draw back the curtain. Tell us for certain - any dream will do." He told them first about the duckling overcoming his fears of the water and though Tom's mind was racing with questions like: 'Why would a duck be scared of water?' and 'Why didn't the mother duck hear its cries?', they managed to discuss sensibly and maturely the issues arising from it.

"Everybody has fears. Arachnophobia is the fear of spiders. Ophidiophobia is the fear of snakes. Anybody know any others?"

"Ergasiophobia," Rob said. "My Head of House says I've got it. Fear of work."

"More like ablutophobia - fear of washing, or tydiophobia - fear of tidying your room."

Ted could have added acrophobia, fear of heights, but resisted the temptation.

"Rational fears are healthy and actually helpful. I'm scared that if I break the speed limit I'll have to pay a fine, or lose my licence."

"Or go on yet another Speed Awareness Course..." Harry added.

"Ok. That's enough. I was just unlucky that they had a speed camera hidden in that horse box."

"But you couldn't have been that frightened or you wouldn't have done it."

"That's my point exactly. If I knew I'd be shot if I was caught I'd be too scared to even contemplate it. Just like at school. If instead of going to the Isolation Room or having a detention you were tortured or executed, behaviour would change overnight."

"Thank you Ted Bin Laden or should it be Adolf Tedler?"

"So are you saying being frightened of death and of God are good things?"

"Logically yes. We should be scared of God and going against His will or our punishment will be eternal damnation if you believe what the bible says."

"Heavy!"

"I know, but that's what this third pillar is all about. Fear of God should lead to reverence and reverence should lead to hating evil and doing wrong and that would make everybody wiser and happier."

"So why are we scared of death if that leads to a better place and eternal happiness? Surely we should actually be looking forward to it?"

"You're right. It makes no sense. That's why we made mum's funeral a celebration - both of her amazing life and legacy, but also of where we hope she is now. No more suffering, illness, vasculitis…"

The four sat in silence for some time, lost in their own memories and thoughts.

"I suppose the Zip Wire today was like that. We all had to overcome our fears of the height or the speed or failure of equipment and we had to do it in our own way. But hey - we all managed it." Harry beamed at the others. Ted glanced at Rob and they both considered how easy it sounded, but how difficult it was. The third pillar was a tough challenge. He shared with them Lawrence's trip to the Holy Land and they sat enthralled as usual.

"Wow! I wonder how this near death experience affected him? He must have learnt a healthy fear of travelling alone and murderous strangers, but he doesn't sound like he learnt to hate evil if he lied to his parents about what happened."

Harry was as matter of fact as usual.

Rob's response was unusually serious and his two siblings looked shocked when he said:

"He was doing that to protect them. Sometimes we need a shield and protector. Sometimes the truth is too painful. Fear can affect you in all sorts of ways, maybe when you least expect it. I agree with dad. A healthy fear is a useful brake and is a help rather than a hindrance."

Tom could think of a thousand witty retorts, but was too shocked to use them. Harry looked at his father, but Ted shook his head.

"Who's for Cranium before bed?" he said to bring them all back to earth with a bump and that was their entertainment for the rest of the evening.

14

"The Fourth Pillar of Wisdom," Ted had read on the ever-reliable Wikipedia website, "is listening to advice and choosing wisely which to act upon."

Ted drifted off to sleep thinking of all the guidance and comfort he had been given over the last few months from counsellors, friends and family.

In his dream he was sitting in a cafe on his own, nursing a cappuccino and trying in vain to look out through the steamed-up windows as the rain lashed down outside, the wind blew dramatically and a storm raged all around.

As he sat waiting for the storm to pass, one by one, mysterious, ghost-like, faceless apparitions came up behind him and whispered in his ear. "Don't try and rush grief. It has its own timetable. Just make sure there are lots of soft places around - pillows, shoulders, arms..."

Then: "Let your tears out. They are a river which will take you somewhere new, lifting you off the rocks."

Another whispered:

"Love and laughter will return - but in the meantime; tears and plenty of chocolate!"

A fourth said:

"Don't feel guilt at grief. Remember, it isn't the absence of love; it isn't loss: it's proof that love is still there; still alive."

Then: "don't bottle it up. Let it out. We want to share your burden and can only do so if you talk about it, however painful for both of us."

"Grief is a hole in the ground. To begin with you'll keep falling in. After a while it will still be there, but at times you'll learn to walk around it."

Finally, just before he awoke, he heard the words:

"Life isn't about waiting for the storm to pass. The great lesson is to dance in the rain."

As he looked around the cafe again, he saw it was now packed with all his family and friends who helped him to his feet and gently, but firmly, pushed him out of the now open door.

It was still raining heavily but it didn't make him wet and as he started to dance a massive rainbow appeared overhead - a promise of sunshine to come and that the worst was behind.

In his second dream, Lawrence was eager to continue his narrative, almost impatient as if he had been waiting a long time.

"Back from the Holy Land, I had to complete my studies at Jesus College and produce my thesis. My personal experiences were a great advantage and I really enjoyed the research and study involved and was extremely proud of the end product, though I did wonder whether it

would be too radical and over-confident for my jury - the academics of Oxford University.

I was pleasantly surprised when I was awarded a first; not that it mattered to me that much, but it would open doors in the next phase of my life.

My thirst for travel and for history were unquenched, despite my near-death experience at Urfa, so I joined up with fellow enthusiasts Hogarth and Thompson and we travelled via the delights of Athens and Constantinople to Carchemish to join an eighty man archaeological dig.

These were to be truly the happiest days of my life: working alongside and constantly learning from men I respected and admired.

I had never been good at taking counsel, whether it be from my parents, friends at college, teachers and lecturers or even famous historians whose opinion I asked such as Charles Doughty.

I was a headstrong, opinionated youth, but in my early twenties I was learning to listen, consider and decide, rather than dive in and bluster my way through life.

Truly this was a pillar of wisdom which I needed in order to mature and develop as a character. It would prove an invaluable tool in the war years to come and would contrast markedly with the blunders and catastrophic errors made by army leaders on all sides.

There were all kinds of rumours circulating about the nature of our presence there, with conspiracy theorists claiming that it was all a Government initiative to keep an eye on the Germans building the railway nearby and to gauge the friendliness of the Turkish government, but for me it was all about unearthing the past and learning from history.

These were lessons that I was to need in my own life. I learnt such a lot from natives and was struck by the irony that foreigners came out to teach and missionaries came out to convert, but ended up learning themselves and being converted to a different culture and way of looking at life.

When the dig finished I could not resist exploring the region to make the most of the opportunity and did so enjoyably until it was time to return to England, vowing to return 'home' as soon as I possibly could.

15

As usual, Harry was up first and on his laptop. Ted surfaced second and Rob and Tom appeared eventually, looking suitably dishevelled and exhausted. They had settled quickly into the holiday routine, grabbing breakfast on the go and then heading into the lounge to check their phones in case anything cataclysmic had happened back home which would now be on Facebook, such as one of their friends having a shower or having to remove a splinter before it caused septicaemia.

It turned out they were missing major world events including Rita Ora buying a new black and white bikini, Gwen Stefani filing for divorce and Kim Kardashian living dangerously by having a wine gum while she was pregnant.

'FOMO' - fear of missing out - could be a real issue, but they would have to soldier on.

Ted cleared his throat teacher-style and held his hand in the air for attention.

"Put phones away please. I don't want to have to confiscate them again."

Some of his students at school needed them to be surgically removed rather than confiscated!

"Today is Thursday - day four of Operation Cymru and Pillar Four as far as our Wisdom Temple is concerned.

That means today's theme is advice - the giving of and receiving. Today our trip is going to be to…"

He paused and the lads obliged with a drum roll on the table.

"…Surf Snowdonia!"

Harry, Rob and Tom cheered and jumped up in excitement. Surf Snowdonia had only been open a few days and everybody at school had been talking about it and wanted to try it out, but it was booked solid for the first two months.

"Wow, dad, you're the man! How have you managed that? Is it an ex-student who owes you a favour? You told us they were all on the dole or in prison!"

"No I've got a mate that works for nPower in Dolgarrog where the Surf Snowdonia has been built and they provide them with the water. David's a scary bloke - six feet five or seven or thirteen - I'm never sure, but anyway, he threatened to withdraw the water supply if they didn't get us in."

The boys were not sure they believed their hyperbole-loving father, but who cared? They were off to Dolgarrog and Surf Snowdonia.

All the way there they sang Beach Boy classics such as 'Surfin' U.S.A.' and 'I Get Around' and 'California Girls' only they'd become 'Surfin' Dolgarrog', 'I run aground' and 'Scousebrow Girls'.

Ted booked them in and went off to park the car. He hoped they had learnt their lesson from the Zip Wire, particularly Rob.

They were chatting away in the queue to all sorts of surfer dudes and everybody was quick to offer advice and sound like an expert.

Even Rob and Tom were more than happy to give advice to some younger children behind them: "Standing on one leg is the best way to balance," Rob was heard to say, "then closing your eyes and singing the Welsh National Anthem."

Tom and Harry smiled, but both hoped that the counsel of Dalai Rob would be ignored.

Ted had a pleasant day in the Lagoon Cafe, sipping coffee and reading the latest Harper Lee novel, 'Go set a watchman'. He thought about all the watchmen and women in his own life who had really been looking out for him and supporting him through the last few months and felt overwhelmed. He had never felt so lonely - but so loved.

The three lads had a whale of a time. Harry obviously listened intently to the instructor's advice and mastered it immediately, standing expertly and riding high on wave after wave.

Rob had learnt from the Zip Wire trauma and was more cautious. He had clearly taken in some of the expert tuition, but still managed some classic wipeouts, though he always surfaced with a broad grin on his face.

Tom loved it - but found it almost impossible to stand. He could belly-board like a pro, but every time he tried to stand he came a cropper. He had too many questions in his head and too many random snippets of 'wise' counsel from the other surfers, so confusion reigned and he struggled accordingly.

Still, all three had the time of their lives and couldn't believe how quickly the day passed. As they headed back to Tremadog and Snowdon Lodge they were all elated - but exhausted.

16

At dinner Ted shared his latest two dreams with them.

They really didn't know what to make of the cafe story, though all three were struck by the relevance of the analogies which had been described.

Harry had made himself busy and so had bottled up his emotions. Anger had been his driving force at first, but the tears had never really flowed so he was challenged by the river illustration.

Rob, who had always been the joker in the pack, had become less so, but he was largely in denial about the whole episode in their lives, so the hole in the ground and reality of it all affected him.

Tom found all the illustrations interesting, but none of them helpful. He still had too many questions that he needed answering and so wasn't ready to move forward.

Ted empathised with all of them. He realised that the reason that he had dreamt them was that they were all rushing around in his head. They were all phrases he had heard, or sympathy cards he had read or analogies explored by therapists.

The secret was to listen to them all; consider and explore them and then adopt them only if they were useful and helpful. He understood the fourth pillar of wisdom now.

"So what did we learn at Surf Snowdonia today?" he ventured.

"That it's amazing, awesome, ace, awe-inspiring, alluring…"

"OK, I get the picture."

"Hang on, I haven't finished 'a' yet and there's twenty five more letters to come."

"Clearly you liked it, but I didn't ask that. What did you learn?"

"To listen to the instructor who knew what he was talking about and take all the other advice with a pinch of salt." Harry's voice of reason rang out in the darkness.

"But surely everybody has an opinion and it's worth listening to?" asked Tom, still confused.

"Yes, like those poor kids who kept wiping out because they were standing on one leg with their eyes closed singing 'Mae hen wlad' as loud as they could," Ted observed and they all laughed.

"Shouldn't have believed me should they? Their own stupid fault. Stupid is as stupid does as the wise seer Gump once said."

"What about Lawrence's story? Do you think he's becoming wiser with age and experience? Hanging around with others of like mind who he really respected must have helped don't you think?"

"Absolutely, maybe that's the key to this pillar. First you have to listen and that's not easy in itself. Then you need to consider and decide who you respect and who knows what they're talking about - so today the instructor, but definitely not Rob."

They all laughed again.

"That's right," Harry added, "sometimes I just want to talk and somebody to listen, and it winds me up when they have come up with a solution. That's not what I need right now."

"But they're only trying to help," Ted suggested, "and if you turn them away and stop talking, or refuse to talk about it at all, that's going to be worse long-term, whether it's exam stress or bullying or bereavement."

They all knew he was right and yet it was all so difficult. Still, they had had a marvellous day and they had all learnt something about themselves, as well as Lawrence, so it was a triple win situation.

17

Ted's dream was even more vivid and memorable that night.

He was in a school and came back to his classroom after break to find that his bag was open and his wallet was next to it, but the money that he had withdrawn from the cash machine that morning was gone.

He could not believe his stupidity at leaving his room unlocked and his bag unattended, but was still angry and felt disappointed that somebody would steal from him. He would never have dreamt of doing so.

It was a double lesson split by a break so when his students returned from fighting off the seagulls who were after their crisps, pies and chocolate bars - their usual healthy diet - he tackled them on the theft, but unsurprisingly, nobody owned up.

He decided to test them so he went into the woodwork area and cut thirty sticks of equal length, telling the students that justice was a powerful force and that the stick of the person who had stolen his money would grow, like Pinocchio's nose, and be two inches longer the next day.

When they came in the next morning they were asked to bring their sticks down to registration and sure enough it had worked.

One student's stick was two inches shorter than all the others because the guilt of his crime meant he had cut it by two inches so it would stay the same length as all the others.

He lectured the class on honesty, justice and the wisdom of behaving in a moral, correct way.

In his second dream, Lawrence continued the account of his life from where he left off.

'Between 1911 and 1913 I spent four exhausting but fascinating seasons, excavating at Carchemish, even finding time to build our own spacious excavation house next to the site.

They were the happiest days of my life and I wish they could have gone on forever. I was being paid to pursue my hobby, living abroad and putting into practice the head knowledge I had gained from my studies at Oxford.

Tragically the rumours and rumblings of an impending war grew and in January 1914 I was co-opted by the British military to undertake a survey of the Neger desert in an area referred to in the bible as the Wilderness of Zin.

This was a remote and yet beautiful area between Elim and Mount Sinai where the Israelites wandered during their exodus, continually turning away from God, but then realising the error of their ways.

Strategically it was vital to all sides in any conflict, as the Ottoman army attacking Egypt would have to cross it, so we were effectively being used as spies to keep an eye on developments and in the meantime map the area identifying water sources and potential bases.

It was a strange experience but it did give me an opportunity to visit Aqaba and the unforgettable

Petra, the most incredible sight I was ever to witness, with its rose-coloured rock and ornate carvings.

When hostilities started in August 1914 I was recalled and sent to Cairo to use my experience, linguistic skill and local knowledge to aid the war effort.

The next four years were to change mine and everybody else's lives.'

18

"Right gentlemen, you have exactly thirty minutes to eat your breakfast and get ready. The limousine - better known as dad's taxi - will be leaving at 9:30 am."

It was Friday and Ted had designed a different day for his sons. Their favourite TV programme was 'The Apprentice' and today he was to be Lord Sugar (or Baron Sweetener as Rob was to call him) and they were to be apprentices for the day.

"I have arranged with Caernarfon Castle that you will spend the morning touring the castle and shadowing the guides and in the afternoon you will be assigned groups of tourists to take round the castle.

You will each be on your own and are not allowed to seek help from the professional guides. You can conduct your tours in any way you choose, but the success of your venture will be judged by the tips you collect.

Back in the boardroom - here, we will count the tips and the one with the least money will be fired."

He pointed his finger and glared at each of them in turn.

"Any questions anyone?"

The boys were stunned. They had been looking forward to exploring Caernarfon Castle but hadn't been expecting to work there!

"What happens to the money? Can we keep it?" asked the ever-optimistic Tom.

"All proceeds will go to our chosen charity - Vasculitis UK - but there will be a secret treat for the winner."

When they got to the castle they separated and each went on an organised tour. They were bombarded with information and facts, lots of head-knowledge, but had to decide how to use it.

'Built by Edward I in only five years' , 'the site of a Roman legend', 'based on Constantinople', 'an hourglass design', 'polygonal towers of 6,8 and 10 sides including the impressive Eagle Tower', 'murder-holes in the huge gateways'…

There was so much to take in, but they had to use it wisely if they were to please their customers and win the challenge.

Harry decided to go for the top end of the market, as he estimated that they were the richest and would give the best tips.

He marketed his tour as 'A Fortress of Facts' and designed a fact sheet for each of his customers giving well-known and lesser known facts about the castle and the town of Caernarfon.

He himself would lead the guided tour and at the end there would be a quiz with a chance to win a key ring with a picture of the castle on it.

Rob went for the more entertaining option and aimed his at a target audience of families. His would be more of a dramatic performance and he dressed up as a court jester and asked his clients to play along by choosing costumes to wear from the 'dressing-up room'.

He figured that if they enjoyed themselves and had a good laugh they would tip him well and if the kids enjoyed it, the parents and grandparents would too. He just hoped that jokes like: 'How do you open a drawbridge? With a re-moat control.' and 'I sleep in the castle once every two weeks - I call it my fort-night.' and worst of all: 'Castles are great places for a party. They've always been famous for their knight-life.', would get a laugh.

It was a gamble but he was confident it would pay off.

Tom went for a multi-activity day for all the family. He found guided tours boring himself, so he organised a range of activities from archery to orienteering around the grounds and 'torture corner' where they could throw sponges at each other in the stocks or try out the thumbscrews.

He figured that people who came to a castle on holiday were active and so the more different opportunities there were, the more memorable their visit would be and so higher tips would be assured.

Ted watched on fascinated. The fifth pillar of wisdom was "sound wisdom" which meant the practical, day-to-day use of what you have learned.

All three looked like good ideas, but none of them had asked for advice (Pillar 4) and conducted market research before launching their tours.

They had definitely gone with their own strengths and expertise, which he knew met with Lord Sugar's approval, and they all had customers, but who would win?

Only the evening and the boardroom would tell.

19

When they walked into the dining room of Snowdon Lodge, they expected a takeaway to be set out on the table, but the layout of the furniture had changed.

Ted had brought the leather armchair in from the lounge and was sitting looking out of the window.

He had pushed the other two tables together and placed three of the upright dining chairs behind it to make it appear as much like the boardroom in 'The Apprentice' as he could.

"Good evening candidates. Take a seat."

The boys had to try hard not to laugh, but they decided to play along and complied silently.

"Right then," Ted Sugar continued, let's talk about each of your ideas first, before we get to the numbers.

Oldest first, tell me Harry what your business plan was."

"Well as the task was all about tips I opted for the high end of the market. I knew I would have less customers, but I also reckoned they would be more generous as they had more expendable income so I would win.

My tours were called 'A Fortress of Facts' and all the adults who signed up were complimentary and seemed satisfied. They enjoyed the educational aspect of the day."

"What about you Rob?" Ted asked.

"I dressed up as a court jester and went for the family market, aiming to entertain rather than educate. Mine was called 'Jolly Jests' and most of my customers actually liked the jokes and had a good laugh.

There was one girl called Bethan who didn't really get them, but that seemed to make them even funnier to the rest."

"Well done. Finally, Tom, what about you?"

"I went for an activity day with lots of different choices for all ages. The archery was popular and the 'Knight Karaoke' where they sang madrigals and re-mixes like 'Drawbridge over Troubled Water' and 'Clap along if you feel like a fort without a roof'. They certainly were happy when they left."

"Interesting and different ideas, but well done to all three of you for your innovative imagination. My only criticism would be that you plunged straight into it without seeking counsel or advice. None of you asked the customers in the morning what they thought of your ideas to gauge interest. On the other hand, the Castle staff were all impressed by the feedback from your customers and all three of you made profit."

He left a long, pregnant pause to build up the tension and for a few minutes the brothers knew exactly how the real contestants must have felt.

"Remember it's all based on total tips rather than total customers. If it was based on numbers of customers, Tom would have won; Rob would be second and Harry third."

Tom was about to launch into a goal celebration but remembered that this wasn't relevant to the task they had been set.

"The results are as follows…The profit from tips for Harry's 'Fortress of Facts' was…£50."

Harry smiled and the other two gasped. How could they beat that? It sounded a lot of money for an afternoon's work.

"The profits from tips for Rob's 'Jolly Jests' was…£50."

A draw - amazing! But would they be equal first or equal second?

"Finally for Tom's 'Fort of Fun', the profit from tips was…£50. So I declare it a draw and for the first week on 'The Apprentice', nobody will be fired and you'll all get a treat. Da iawn. Well done to one and all."

The boys high-fived but were confused.

"Are you sure dad? It seems a bit of a coincidence that we all made exactly the same amount."

"We'll never know. When I went in to collect the tips, the manager said he was so impressed by all three ideas that he planned to introduce all of them in the next programme.

He thought they all had their merits so he wanted you all to be equal winners - no losers. He wanted to give all the tips plus a donation to charity so £150 divided by three was his decision. I'm so proud of all of you."

Normally the competitive streak of the boys would have insisted on pursuing it further, but it did not seem appropriate.

Besides, they had used their practical skills to have a fun day out and raise £150 for Vasculitis UK, so they all voted it the best day of the holiday so far.

20

The Chinese take away from the Happy Chop Suey House arrived and smelt delicious, so their deliberations were interrupted.

Crispy duck was the family favourite and was devoured in seconds by the starving, would-be entrepreneurs and then various side dishes of crispy seaweed and noodles accompanied mouth-watering sweet and sour chicken, chilli beef with black bean sauce, barbecue ribs, pork balls in batter and lots and lots of prawn toast.

Ted shared with them his two dreams of the previous night. The surreal nature of his classroom dream spooked them somewhat and they really didn't know what to make of it.

Harry was struck by the dishonesty of the whole episode and couldn't go much beyond that.

Rob and Tom were more intrigued by the solution and exposure of the crime and Tom as usual posed the more challenging questions.

"Where does our conscience come from? It's never been revealed in any medical examination so what is it?"

They decided to consult the dictionary for clarification.

"The inner sense of what is right or wrong in one's conduct or motives, impelling one toward right action. Moral judgement may derive from values, principles or rules."

"So to have sound wisdom, according to our fifth pillar, you have to behave and act in a right, just and honest way."

"But who decides what is right? Vegetarians say killing animals for food is wrong and it is against their conscience to eat meat, but carnivores like us…", he pointed at the evidence of the scraps of takeaway on the table, "don't agree."

"I suppose that's where wisdom comes in," answered Ted

"It's listening to all the alternatives, reasoning them out and then making a rational judgement."

They went on to discuss Lawrence's experiences as an archaeologist and now a spy for the British army.

"I'll bet he struggled with his conscience," Harry commented. "It sounds from what we've heard that he was an academic and archaeologist who had really identified with the Arab way of life.

The thought that his information might lead to war and the death of countless Arabs must have made it difficult to sleep at night."

Ted thought about the countless sleepless nights he had experienced since losing Rosie and the rollercoaster emotions of guilt, despair and fear he had endured. Then the stabbing thrusts of his conscience if he had a fun day or forgot for a while. He had read the Christina Rossetti poem and understood the sentiment of the words: 'If you should forget me for a while and afterwards remember, do not grieve. Better by far you should forget and smile than that you should remember and be sad', but logic and reasoning were overwhelmed by raw emotion and conscience. If only there was an off switch for the brain as well as the TV, he had often thought.

"How is he going to cope when war does break out?" Tom asked. "How will his conscience cope with that?"

"Spoiler alert!" Rob shouted. "Now you've given away the next part of the story."

They all laughed and Harry reminded them of a friend at school who had been upset when his media teacher, Mrs Delacoe, had 'ruined' Titanic for him by revealing the ending. He had even suggested there should be a sequel - 'Titanic 2' or 'Return of Titanic', much to the amusement of the rest of the class.

"War never solves anything," Ted added, "The First World War is a case in point. How can anybody seriously call it the 'Great War'? Over nine million people dead." It was a gross over-simplification, but they empathised with the sentiment nonetheless.

"Why didn't he refuse to serve? If all the soldiers had done the same they couldn't have shot them all for being conscientious objectors surely?"

"That's the strange thing Tom," Ted replied. "They were following their conscience. They genuinely believed that what they were doing was for the good of their families and their country. They believed they were fighting evil and upholding good. 'For God and country' was one of their catchphrases."

"How bizarre!" Rob was stunned.

"What about the word 'sound'? It's come to mean popular, accepted. Sound as a pound."

"Originally it meant healthy or in good condition; then good judgement and able to be trusted." Ted was in teacher-mode.

"So I wonder if Lawrence gave sound advice to the British Government or his view was slanted by his personal experiences? It'll be interesting to watch the film again now we know all the background."

"Funny you should say that." Ted produced a DVD from a carrier bag by the table.

"Look what I found in the Bargain Box at Poundland before we came - thought it might come in handy."

Rob couldn't resist the question.

"How much was it? It was a sound bargain I hope. Sound for a pound in Poundland."

They tidied up the remains of the Chinese and settled down to 227 minutes of Peter O'Toole, Alec Guinness, Omar Sharif and Anthony Quinn re-enacting the next part of Lawrence's life.

21

As a result of watching the film immediately before bedtime, Ted's dreams were even more dramatic than usual.

In his first dream, he himself was the central character. It was one of those dreams where you were aware you were dreaming, but couldn't properly wake up to end it.

It was based on the plot of Disney's latest film 'Inside Out', but in Ted's version, he took the place of Riley and the five emotions battling it out for control of his mind were Joy, Sadness, Fear, Guilt and Anger.

Just like in the film, Anger, Guilt, Sadness and Fear took it in turns to control his mind; his Headquarters, while Joy was away on holiday.

It was all a confused, terrifying nightmare until Joy finally returned with a new remote control which could mute Anger, Guilt and Fear and work together with Sadness to build a new and different Headquarters.

He woke up in a cold sweat aware it had been a nightmare, but also aware that this had been a pretty close re-enactment of the past six months of his life.

Ted forced himself to focus on other thoughts and particularly the 'Lawrence of Arabia' film and when he finally got back to sleep, he heard the voice of Lawrence again.

"1914 to 1918 were the most traumatic and dramatic years in history and everybody who lived through them, or lost loved ones, would never be the same again.

For some reason I have been painted as a war hero and my legacy has been drawn from the Hollywood representation of my exploits.

Indeed, it started immediately after the war when I became a celebrity due to the photo show and lecture launched in 1919 by Lowell Thomas entitled 'With Allenby in Palestine and Lawrence in Arabia'.

I hated the publicity and glamorisation of what had been horrendous years. I was an academic and archaeologist first; explorer second and soldier last, if at all.

All my efforts were to minimise bloodshed and support my friends the Arabs, but my portrayal as a dashing hero charging into battle on the back of a camel were all that was to be remembered of me.

I gave my full account in 'Seven Pillars of Wisdom', but again this became a journal of war, rather than what was intended - a book about developing character, understanding and wisdom.

I also served in 1921 as an advisor to Winston Churchill, counselling him on the dangers of war and how important it was to avoid it at all costs.

By 1922 I had had enough of being public property and recognised everywhere I went, so I changed my name to John Hume Ross and enlisted in the RAF in the hope of travelling the world again.

It was my third surname. I would always be known as T. E. Lawrence; but I had been born Chapman and now took the name Ross, so LCR rather than TEL or

LOA for Lawrence of Arabia, would be more accurate.

To confuse matters further, my first name was Thomas, but I was always known to my friends as Ned.

I wanted to disappear and become invisible, but my war record and the lecture tour and my books made this impossible and scandal and gossip pursued me for the next few years even while I was stationed in India on the other side of the world.

I purchased some plots of land and settled in Chingford and tried to visit as often as I could and settled for a number of years in Bridlington, Yorkshire serving in the RAF and enjoying high speed adventures in planes, boats and motorcycles."

22

"Come on kids! Get a move on! We've got to be out of here in fifteen minutes or we'll miss the boat."

It was Saturday and day six of their holiday and an early start if they were to complete the forty minute drive to Porth Meudwy, near Aberdaron, in order to catch the early ferry to Bardsey Island.

They had had many highlights of their holiday already, but this was to be a special day which they had looked forward to for ages.

Ted and Rosie's friends Steve and Jo had "emigrated" to Bardsey several years ago and their children Ben and Rachel had been particularly missed by Rob and Tom.

Holidays in Beaumaris and Denbigh had brought them close, but this time they were almost on the doorstep and even though it would be bitter-sweet without Rosie, as every new adventure was, it was on everybody's bucket list, as it had been for thousands of pilgrims for hundreds of years.

The crossing was notoriously tricky due to the currents in the Sound, but Colin the skipper made it entertaining and the range of geology in the rocks and sight of the dolphins and a vast array of seabirds including gannets, guillemots and razorbills made the time go quickly.

Once landed, they headed for the farmhouse to surprise Steve, Jo, Ben and Rachel and the shrieks of joy reverberated round the island and could probably be heard on the mainland.

They had an amazing day exploring the island which was only 1 1/2 miles long at its widest point and just over half a mile across, but seemed vast.

They roamed around the farmland and climbed the 167 metre mountain which straddled the island.

Harry was fascinated by the incredible history of the place and genuinely felt like he was walking in the footsteps of countless pilgrims who had visited faithfully right since the sixth century when it was believed that St. Cadfan had begun building the monastery. The Abbey ruins also captured his imagination.

Rob enjoyed the lighthouse - thirty metres in height and the tallest square-towered lighthouse in the UK. He ran up and down the stairs several times, racing Ben and Rachel who beat him every time and relished a new audience for his jokes, such as 'How do lighthouse keepers communicate? Shine language' and 'What instrument do lighthouse keepers play? The fog horn' and worst still: 'What did the ocean say to the lighthouse? Nothing. It just waved.' Ben and Rachel laughed politely and Ted, Harry and Tom were relieved that they had been spared for once.

Tom loved the wildlife. They spent ages watching the seals basking on the rocks and he lost count of the number of species of birds they observed, though he made a note to impress his teacher Miss Jackson with the rare Cretzschmar's Bunting that they watched.

Ted just loved the company and walking with and chatting to Steve and Jo about happy days when they were youth workers together and organised games of 'Captain's Coming' and 'Ladders' and trips to Greenwood Activity Park and Nefyn.

They were the perfect couple to re-assure him that Rosie was enjoying similar walks in heaven; organising games and probably interrogating Newton about how gravity and the moon affect the tides and speaking fifty different languages all at once.

As they waved goodbye and left Bardsey they all felt enriched by their day out, but realised each in their own way, the importance of people to make a special day even more special.

Ted felt like Anger, Guilt and Fear were present but had been muted in the background and, maybe; just maybe Joy had returned.

23

The evening meal was a particularly animated and lively one. Ted had decided to cook which had caused consternation in his loved ones, but actually it was edible, palatable and even tasty. His signature dish had always been 'haricots sur pain grillé' or 'beans on toast' as it was more commonly known, but he had been more adventurous recently and tonight's gastronomic delights were leek and potato soup as a starter, sea bass with mussels for main and his very own strawberry trifle as a dessert.

He shared the dreams of the previous night with them and they all agreed that the plot of 'Inside Out' had had relevance in each of their lives recently.

Harry opened up to share his battle with Anger and how it had eaten away at him over the last few months. He had been forced to keep himself busy to take his mind off his grief, but found himself getting frustrated and cross at the smallest things, particularly when he was driving. Why didn't the driver in front indicate until just before they turned off? Why did a tractor always have to pull out in front of him?

Rob admitted that Fear was his particular issue. He had been frightened to open up and talk about his feelings and so had reverted to his usual jokes and quips in order to hide them.

Tom didn't have one particular trait, but was really mixed up. He had so many unanswered questions and was so confused that he had moments, even hours of Anger, Sadness and Fear and only very occasional glimpses of Joy which were all too fleeting.

They all agreed that the experiences of the holiday had really helped and the big thing was to talk more about how they felt rather than bottle it up inside like a volcano waiting to erupt or a tsunami of fears about to crash on the rocks.

"The sixth pillar of wisdom is understanding", Ted commented. "Maybe we've all come to a better understanding of ourselves this week as well as had an enjoyable time."

"There are so many things we don't understand and accepting that is hard." added Harry. "What do you think of Lawrence's version of the war compared to the film we saw last night?"

"It fascinates me," Tom had his journalist hat on," how the papers or a film can totally influence our view without us realising it. I'll always see Lawrence of Arabia, or should it be Chapman of Tremadog or Ross of India, as a 6 feet 5 inches towering giant and war hero when he really was 5 feet 5 inches and anti-war.

"It certainly seems that way," Ted replied. "I share his sentiments about the war. It was such a waste of lives and it never solves anything. Lawrence was 26 when the war started and in the prime of his life. It must have been difficult afterwards. Sounds like he never felt comfortable with celebrity status and resorted to high speed adrenaline kicks to get by."

"That's why the sixth pillar of wisdom must have been the most difficult for him. Other people didn't really understand him and believed the media persona to be the real one. He wanted to be different but wasn't allowed to be."

"I think we all found that at school in our own way," Harry suggested. "'Dare to be different', we were told but it was much easier to comply and follow the crowd rather than lead them. I remember in Psychology being struck by Fromm's view that we should never explain our actions in order to be understood or approved of. As long as our acts don't hurt anybody else we should answer only to ourselves and our reason and conscience. That's the only way we can be free and make a difference in the world."

"Lawrence certainly had an impact and made a difference, but his legacy wasn't what he would have hoped for or wanted."

"Unlike mum…" Tom added and they all thought of the hundreds of cards and comments in the Book of Memories which were testament to the difference Rosie had made in so many people's lives.

"And if we raise shed loads of money for Vasculitis UK and they find a cure, what a legacy that would be.

Now off to bed. Last day tomorrow and who knows what exciting surprises that will hold. Sweet dreams."

24

Ted himself had mixed dreams.

In the first one he was driving the school minibus through North Wales, but instead of a group of lively, excited school kids, it was packed to the rafters with all his friends and family on a Grand Day Out.

His three sons were in the front with him chatting away, but as he looked in his mirror he could see dozens of faces - relatives, friends and colleagues from school.

He was puzzled by how many passengers he had and was becoming nervous and uneasy. Suddenly a thick fog descended and he slowed down peering forwards as best he could. Whenever he suggested stopping and waiting for the fog to clear there was a chorus from his family and friends urging him on.

"Keep going Ted! It'll clear soon. We're all with you!"

It was a winding, twisty road and he could vaguely make out 'Criccieth 4 miles' then 'Criccieth 3 miles' as they moved agonisingly, slowly onwards.

He was desperate to stop, give in and turn back, but there was no way he would be allowed to. Cars and huge lorries kept shooting past going in the opposite direction, but somehow they avoided collisions by the skin of their teeth.

After what seemed like forever, the minibus started to climb a steep hill and he peered into the gloom to see 'Criccieth 1 mile.'

For the first time on the journey he genuinely believed that they were going to make it and as he did so everybody in the minibus started to sing at the top of their voices.

"Walk on, walk on with hope in your heart and you'll never walk alone. You'll never walk alone."

The hairs on the back of Ted's neck stood up and his spine tingled just like they always did when he heard The Kop anthem belted out and at that very moment they reached the top of the hill and emerged from the pea-souper fog into glorious sunshine with Criccieth Castle glinting ahead of them.

It was a view that he knew Rosie had loved above all others and he sensed that she was there with them too, smiling and singing.

Everybody in the minibus went silent, stunned by the beauty of the vista and all that could be heard was a single bird trilling a song which echoed from the hills around them. It was a skylark and its sweet, silver song filled the air as it soared ever higher and higher.

For the first time in months Ted smiled. Somebody behind him was reciting Shelley's 'Ode to a skylark':

"Higher still higher
From the earth thou springest,
Like a cloud of fire;
The blue deep thou wingest,
And singing still dost soar, and soaring ever singest.
Teach me half the gladness
That thy brain must know;
Such harmonious madness
From my lips would flow,
The world should listen,
as I am listening now."

Ted knew in his heart that the message was for him primarily, but he also became aware that it was for all the passengers in the minibus who were hurting too.

He became aware of another sound, getting louder and louder and louder. It was a cuckoo calling and it woke him up with a start.

25

For once Ted went back to sleep almost immediately and saw the vision of Lawrence/Chapman/Ross very clearly.

"I had never courted fame or celebrity status, but somehow I had become one. My part in the war and in particular the Arab revolt and sieges of Aqaba and Damascus would stick long in people's memories and were to be encapsulated in an Oscar-winning feature film, but that was the direct opposite of what I had hoped and prayed my legacy would be.

My books 'Seven Pillars of Wisdom' and 'Revolt in the Desert' and the unfinished 'The Mint' tried to tell the true story, but to no avail.

I worked tirelessly for the Arab cause and was devastated and demoralised by the partitioning settlement which my fellow countrymen agreed on.

I was offered a knighthood and Victoria Cross by the King, but declined them, viewing them as the ultimate example of hypocrisy if I accepted.

To set the record straight and present some real facts instead of Hollywood fantasy - I was 5 feet 5 inches tall; illegitimate; a vegetarian and teetotaller all my life and I loved travel, archaeology and speed.

Most important of all - and the real dramatic climax of my life story - I was murdered.

The official account is that on May 13th 1935, I was out riding my Brough motorcycle near my cottage, Clouds Hill in Dorset, when I came to a dip in the road. As I came up the rise I encountered two young boys on bicycles. Swerving, I lost control and was flipped over the handlebars of my motorbike, sustaining a fatal head injury from which I died six days later.

This was how it was portrayed at the inquest and in the newspapers and it was said that 'All of Britain mourned his passing' and Winston Churchill said that "we had lost one of the greatest beings alive in this time."

All very fascinating, but rumours of a conspiracy theory and cover-up have abounded ever since so I want to set the record straight, once and for all.

I was assassinated due to my political leanings and alliances. It is well-known that I was hired as a spy before and after the war, but this also carried on afterwards.

I was horrified by my experiences in the war, as millions of others were who refused to talk about them, but I had influence.

I aligned myself with Sir Oswald Moseley, leader of the British Union of Fascists and on that fateful day I was actually on my way to see Henry Williamson who was working to arrange a meeting with Adolf Hitler.

I was appalled by the rumours of another impending world war and felt that negotiation with Hitler, rather than antagonising him and alienating him was the only way forward.

I wanted my legacy to be preventing another war, rather than being a 'hero' from the first one, but it was not to be.

There was a real active war lobby in England, God only knows why, and if I spoke up on behalf of the peace movement they saw this as a dangerous initiative.

I was indeed on that Dorset road, but there were no cyclists on that day. A mysterious black car appeared in my mirrors and as I pulled over to let it pass it swerved and knocked me flying over the handlebars.

Conjecture, you say. Where's the proof? Well four witnesses stated they saw a car, including a delivery man and a soldier, one Private Catchpole. But none of them gave evidence at the inquest which was held coincidentally, or not, at Bovington Camp controlled by MI5, instead of a local court.

Indeed Catchpole himself mysteriously died shortly afterwards. Who was in the car? Why was it on that road? Who hired the assassins?

These are questions that investigators need to answer. Some say Winston Churchill himself ordered MI5 to carry out the murder, but no papers exist to prove or disprove this.

I leave you with one fact; one vital piece of evidence which was not used in the inquest, but is documented and recorded.

When Brough Motorcycles examined their top-of-the-range motorcycle to check for a fault, why was there black paint on the outside of the handlebars proving high impact with a car; not tarmac or fields?

I had hoped my legacy would be to help my fellow countrymen to learn from history, see sense and avoid another disastrous episode, but alas that was not to be.

Ironically, though, fate did take a hand and something positive did come out of my untimely and tragic death.

I had not been wearing a crash helmet that day, but as a result of my "accident" and fatal brain and head injuries, a law was passed thanks to research by Hugh Cairns, a neurosurgeon, and so my death has effectively saved thousands of lives.

So at least my story which had had so many ups and downs and twists and turns ends on a happier note.

26

You could have knocked Ted down with the smallest feather ever recorded when he ambled into the dining room the following morning.

There was a phrase at work which had become almost folklore of 'Last day's last day', but this last morning of the holidays was to be unforgettable right from the first moment.

His three sons were all up and dressed and were sitting at the table waiting for him. Breakfast was made, the table had been set.

He pinched himself hard. Was this a third dream or could it really be happening?

"OK, what have you done? Rob, what have you broken? Tom, who have you upset? Harry, how much money do you need?"

"Charming!" chorused the boys. "We decided that you deserved a treat today. You spend your whole life thinking of others - educating the unwilling students; counselling the stressed ones; placating stroppy parents and this week planning surprises for us. So today's your turn."

"Twenty minutes before we have to leave, so tuck in!"

Ted felt strangely nervous, hoping that Harry had taken charge of arrangements as he feared Rob's strange sense of humour or Tom's thirst for adventure might lead to him bungee jumping from Menai Bridge or white water rafting down the Conwy River.

Thankfully Harry was in charge.

"Straight after breakfast we're going to jump in the car and today I'm driving. We're going to Rhos on Sea and it'll take about 40 minutes. That's where your grand day out will begin."

"Rhos-on-Sea? What's there?"

"You'll see. Now stop arguing and get a move on."

The role reversal was strangely surreal.

The drive to Rhos was scenic. They headed across The Cob, through Porthmadog and then up and over the spectacular Crimea Pass through Betws-y-Coed and Llanrwst, then on to the A55 to the coast.

He had no idea what lay ahead and still didn't when they parked and walked down the promenade.

Ahead lay cafes and a pub, the Rhos Fynach, and a fun-looking, brand new crazy golf course. The boys pretended to walk past, then doubled back and through the gates of the mini golf course.

Ted couldn't help himself. "Is that it? We've come all this way for a game of crazy golf? There's one in Porthmadog you know?"

"That's true," Harry said. "But we decided on this one and we're competing for this…" With a flourish he produced a tiny trophy from his pocket with 'Krazy Cup' inscribed on it.

Ted was impressed but still seriously underwhelmed.

"And even though you fancy your chances because they are 1 in 4; I'm afraid the odds are actually 1 in 19…"

Simultaneously to the word "nineteen", familiar faces appeared from the shrubbery, the cafe windows and behind him.

"Surprise!" they shouted and Tom certainly was!

Friends and relatives and work colleagues, all of whom had been on the minibus in his dream, hugged him and shook his hand and thrust a pink ball into one hand and a putter into the other.

"On the tee, from Liverpool, Ted Gobsmacked!" Rob did his best impression of Ivor Robson, the First Tee announcer at the British Open.

Tad was too emotionally drained and shell shocked to play well - well, that was his excuse at any rate, but he loved the banter and relished the challenges of Hole 3 'The Squid' and Hole 6 'The Pirate's Skull' and best of all, Hole 9 ' The Wave' with its fearsome ramp.

This was his kind of challenge - much better than bungee jumping or white-water rafting.

It was a perfect day for Ted. Crazy golf followed by lunch at Fortes in Rhos, then a stroll along the prom and pier in Llandudno for the adults and toboggan or ski slope for the active and the arcade for the less thrill-seeking.

Then it was on to Conwy and 'The Mulberry' for a meal together and Ted was impressed by the views of the marina, the tastiness of the food and the amazing service given by Luke, a young waiter who managed to cope with the demands of a table for nineteen and still retain a smile. Ted even considered a tip - but only for a fraction of a nanosecond!

He had often wondered how he would be able to thank all those people who had stood by him and supported him through the dark days of Rosie's illness, struggle with reactive arthritis and vasculitis, hospitalisation and tragic death, but this was the perfect opportunity to do so.

He also felt the timing was right and though he knew that there were still impossible days ahead, he now felt more equipped to face them.

It had been an incredible holiday full of busy days and new experiences for him and the three lads, but he had learnt a lot.

Lawrence's story was fascinating and he was determined to find out more and investigate the truth about his death. He was also determined to galvanise himself, his family, school and everybody he could, to raise money for Vasculitis UK to find an early intervention and cure for that dreaded disease, so Rosie's legacy would be to help others and save lives.

Most important of all, he had began to build the future on the six pillars of wisdom - prudence to learn self-restraint and sound judgement; knowledge to plan and look ahead rather than always looking backwards; fear of God to produce reverence and good decision making; listening to counsel and giving sound advice; practical sound wisdom to act in a just and right way; developing understanding and acceptance; all of which would eventually provide the seventh pillar, the strength and power to move forward and make a real contribution in the world again.

He knew how tough it was going to be, but as he glanced around 'The Mulberry' at the amazing individuals around him, he knew that he had more than one crutch to lean on. There were eighteen here and countless more who he had been blessed with.

'You can choose your friends, but not your family,' he had heard said, but if he had billions of pounds to spend in the transfer window he could not possibly have done any better than this dream team.

The bill was paid; the trophy presented, to Rob of all people, and they said their fond farewells and headed back for their last night at Snowdon Lodge before heading home.

27

By the time the four of them got back to Snowdon Lodge it was very late and they all headed straight for bed.

For the first time in ages, Ted went straight off to sleep the minute his head touched the pillow and when he woke up he had either not had dreams, or more likely couldn't remember them.

It was a leisurely breakfast as they had to pack, tidy up and leave by 11 o'clock so there was no point in rushing.

He thanked the boys for his treat and shared with them the dreams he had had the previous night.

They were all struck by the 'coincidence' of the connection between the minibus dream and the family gathering and Ted shared his thoughts and emotions at the meal when he had genuinely felt the love and support in the room.

"The end of the Lawrence story was a bombshell," said Harry. "I really didn't see that coming. How much truth do you think there is in the conspiracy theory?"

"Who knows? We need to look into it more when we get home. An important lesson for us, though, was about legacy. When I booked this holiday I wasn't sure it was the right thing. Wales has so many happy memories, but bitter-sweet at the moment."

"It's been awesome dad, thanks. It could only have been bettered if mum had been here too, but I think we've all accepted now that, as much as we wish she could be, she's gone."

Rob and Tom nodded in agreement.

Ted reached into his pocket and unfolded the piece of paper he always carried with him.

"Maybe it's time to read the poem again. When I read it at the funeral it was like an out-of-body experience. I was watching myself read, but it wasn't really me - or about us. Now it really is."

He took a deep breath and read:

"You can shed tears because she's gone
or you can smile because she has lived.
You can close your eyes and pray that she'll come
back
or you can open your eyes and see all she's left.
Your heart can be empty because you can't see her
or you can be full of the love you shared.
You can turn your back on tomorrow and live
yesterday
or you can be happy for tomorrow because of
yesterday.
You can remember her and only that she's gone
or you can cherish her memory and let it live on.
You can cry and close your mind,
be empty and turn your back
or you can do what she'd want:
smile, open your eyes, love and go on."

When he had finished reading he looked up and all three boys were smiling - real smiles for the first time.

"Group hug!" Rob shouted and they embraced for what seemed like hours.

"Mum's legacy of love is in every one of those cards we received and every one of those messages in the Book of Memories and that's what really matters." Ted commented.

"And I'm going to do sponsored walks like Lawrence," said Harry.

"And I'm going to do sponsored bike rides, swims and keepie uppies," said Rob.

"And cake sales and bring and buy sales at school," said Tom.

"And all the money is going to Vasculitis UK so those researchers in Birmingham can crack that horrible disease and mum's legacy will be of spreading love and saving lives."

Ted smiled proudly at his three sons.

"All the pillars of wisdom seem to be in place. Good judgement to decide what we should do; plans for how to move forward and not keep looking back; identifying the evil and vowing to fight it; sharing good advice and relying on the knowledge of the researchers; practical solutions as to how to raise money using our own talents; understanding what the future should hold and the legacy should be and now the power and strength to see it through."

"I always thought you had to be old to be wise," Rob commented "but maybe not."

"I studied the classics at school; I'm that old," Ted added "and remember a saying of Aristotle that 'knowing yourself is the beginning of all wisdom'."

"To succeed in life you need three things - a wishbone, a backbone and a funny bone."

The other three stared at Rob in amazement. Surely he hadn't changed that much during the week and so deeply they hadn't noticed?

"Speaking of which, did you know that Lawrence of Arabia's camel was called Humpfree because it had an extra hump."

Ted, Harry and Tom laughed loud and long. A lot had changed during their week in Tremadog, but at least some things were the same.

The End

Author's Note

This is the fourth novella in a series of six.

The first, HDQ, is about William Davies and was inspired by a trip to Beaumaris Castle.

The second, TOL, is about Edward Jones and was triggered by a trip to the Tower of London.

2014's third novella was AKA and followed a visit to Denbigh and seeing the statue of Henry Morton Stanley on the High Street.

This fourth instalment began with a chance comment about the 1962 classic 'Lawrence of Arabia' and the fact that he was actually born in Tremadog, near Porthmadog.

My wife Lydia and I had begun researching it and discussing it when our lives were turned upside down. I guess they will never be the right way up again.

At Christmas (2014) Lydia felt tired and jaded and alarm bells rang when she was unable to visit her beloved 101 year old mother, but had to go to bed to rest on Christmas Day, of all days.

She was diagnosed with 'a virus' which laid her low and developed into reactive arthritis which was horrendous for her and all those who loved and cared for her.

The arthritis spread through her body causing swollen legs so she couldn't walk; painful swollen arms so she couldn't sleep and even worse boils on her scalp and a swollen jaw so she couldn't eat.

Three long, dark months passed and after many false dawns and hopes of recovery were dashed, she was diagnosed with vasculitis, a rare blood infection which causes the immune system to attack itself, meaning that vital organs are at risk.

With Lydia it was her kidneys and she was rushed to Glan Clwyd with kidney failure. Dialysis and plasma transfer followed and the care of the doctors and nurses was truly amazing, particularly those in the Dialysis Unit who do a remarkable job.

Tragically and catastrophically she suffered a fatal brain haemorrhage and died on April 2nd 2015.

Writing those words is the hardest thing I will ever do and I miss her so much.

For that reason the idea for this book was shelved and nearly abandoned forever, but thanks to friends, work colleagues and family I decided to soldier on.

As an English teacher I have taught about catharsis, the purging of emotion, and never really experienced it, but I can honestly say I have now.

There are three main reasons for publishing this novella:

First for myself to deal with some of the issues which have all but destroyed me in the last six months and try to share them.

Secondly, I hope you enjoy the story of Lawrence and find the ideas of the Seven Pillars of Wisdom interesting and challenging.

Thirdly; little is currently known about the causes and treatment of vasculitis and this must change.

All proceeds from the sales of LCR will go to Vasculitis UK and all other donations would be greatly appreciated.

For more information Vasculitis UK have a website or better still, contact me on my Twitter account @TimMoxley to let me know what you think of LCR.

I was blessed to be a part of a 31 year feel-good story of happiness and adventure and romance which had the most tragic and horrific ending imaginable. Let's change the ending together and make Lydia's legacy a positive one.

Acknowledgements

My heartfelt thanks to all these special people

To LCR Lydia Christina Rose thanks for saying yes to my bumbling proposal in January 1983 and giving me 31 amazing years; the best years of my life.

To Andy and Annwen for their love and support and for using their talents and expertise to convert this handwritten scribble into the professional published version and to Mary and Ann for their proofreading prowess.

To all those friends and family who have carried me through the long, dark days of 2015 particularly Ann, Rod, Geraint and Ioan who went far beyond the call of friendship and sat with me hour after hour in the relatives' room at the hospital while we awaited confirmation of the inevitably tragic news.

To David and Ruth who have lived every moment of the illness and bereavement with me and fed me, comforted me and supported me tirelessly.

To everybody who came to the funeral and the reception. It was heart-warming to see All Saints, Deganwy packed and the RSPB Reserve full to bursting to celebrate together Lydia's life.

To all my friends and family for their visits, phone calls, texts and cards. I am truly blessed with the most wonderful Supporters Club in the world. A particular thanks to Barry and Rod, my brothers and best friends, and to John and Alma, Paul and Michelle, Anne, Rob and Stephen, Ian, Bronwyn, Jim and Sarat, Mike and Diane, Denis and Mavis, Frank and Louise, Dave and Maureen, Kevin and Helen, Naomi and Sam, Diane and Claire and Carolyn who phone me so regularly and faithfully that their phone bills must be astronomical.

To Phil, Sue and everybody at Prestatyn High School where I have been privileged enough to work for the last twenty years. I always knew it was a special place full of amazing people and this year has certainly confirmed it.

Thanks to Liz and Julie who made my absence easier.

To Becky the best Deputy, colleague and friend you could hope for. You must have been taught well!

To Linda, Ella, Tracey, Tricia, Bev, Ben, Jemma, Simon and Gemma in the longsuffering, hardworking English Department. Colleagues and friends - one and all.

To Ceri, Dai, John, Sean, Eins, Lucy, Emma, Liane, Claire and Christina and so many others who sent me texts with words of encouragement and passed me tissues when I wasn't coping.

To everybody at All Saints Church, Deganwy especially Pam, Jeff, Denis, Mavis and Ann who have been constant in prayer and love.

To Marie, Liam, Jen, Peter, Anthony, Helen, Rob, Holly, Steven, Becky and James for visiting me and lifting my spirits, but how could you let Rod take the Krazy Cup home?

To Clare and all the Resources team and Sarah and Faye in the library for their enthusiasm and help.

To Ant, Naomi, Dan, Tom, Kevin, Mark, Charis, Geraint, Ioan, David, Sue, Peter, Margaret, Ann, Grace, Ian, Andy, Annwen and Crethel my 102 year old mother-in-law; friends as well as nephews, nieces and in-laws.

To all the doctors and nurses at Glan Clwyd Hospital especially Julie, Nerys, Ramil, Emma, Liane, Lisa and Jay in the Dialysis Unit who do an amazing job. Da iawn.

Thanks to everybody who has bought and read this book. Please donate.

Finally thanks to Nelson for warming my lap and my heart.

Chapters

You have been reading:

LCR

Also by the same author:

AKA

TOL

HDQ

14260955R00086

Printed in Great Britain
by Amazon.co.uk, Ltd.,
Marston Gate.